I. Introduction

A. Overview of the Artificial Intelligence Market

B. Understanding AI

C. The Business of AI

D. Investing in AI

E. Making Money & Investment with AI

F. Conclusion

II. Understanding AI

A. Definition of Artificial Intelligence

B. Types of AI and their Applications

C. The History and Evolution of AI

D. The Current State of AI and its Impact on Society

III. The Business of AI

A. AI Startups and Emerging Technologies

B. AI and the Job Market

C. AI in Different Industries

D. AI as a Service: Opportunities for Entrepreneurs

IV. Investing in AI

A. Introduction to AI Investing

B. The AI Investment Landscape

C. Choosing the Right AI Companies to Invest In

D. Navigating Risks and Challenges in AI Investing

V. Making Money with AI

A. Monetizing Your Skills with AI

B. AI in Affiliate Marketing and Online Advertising

C. AI and E-commerce: Building an AI-Powered Online Store

D. AI in Software Tech: Opportunities for Investors

VI. Conclusion

A. Recap of the Potential for Making Money with AI in 2023

B. The Future of AI and its Impact on the Global Economy

C. Final Thoughts and Recommendations.

Introduction

A. Overview of the Artificial Intelligence Market

The Artificial Intelligence (AI) market has seen significant growth in recent years and is expected to continue to expand in the coming years. The market is valued at over $100 billion and covers a range of industries, including healthcare, finance, retail, transportation, and more.

One of the major drivers of growth in the AI market is the development of AI-powered products and services, such as chatbots for customer service and intelligent financial management systems for banks. Another growth area is the creation of AI-powered tools and platforms for businesses, including marketing tools and project management platforms.

However, there are also challenges that businesses must overcome to be successful in the AI market. One of the biggest challenges is the shortage of AI talent, as the rapid growth of the industry has led to a shortage of people with the skills and expertise to develop and implement AI solutions. Businesses must be willing to invest in training and development to build a competent AI team.

Another challenge is the need for businesses to ensure the ethical and responsible use of AI, as AI raises significant ethical and privacy concerns. Businesses must ensure that they are using AI in a responsible manner and that they are protecting the privacy and data of their customers.

Investing in AI presents both opportunities and challenges for businesses, and it is important for businesses to understand these opportunities and challenges in order to make informed decisions about their AI strategy. Whether you are a startup or an established business, investing in AI and developing a strategy to leverage its power can help you stay ahead of the competition and achieve long-term success.

page break

Understanding AI

Artificial Intelligence (AI) has been a subject of interest and innovation for decades, with its roots dating back to the 1950s. It has since then evolved into a rapidly growing field that is transforming many aspects of our lives. In this section, we will discuss what AI is, how it works, and its various applications.

A. What is Artificial Intelligence?

Artificial Intelligence, or AI, is a field of computer science that focuses on creating machines and computer programs that can perform tasks that typically require human intelligence, such as recognizing speech, making decisions, and solving problems. The goal of AI is to create systems that can perform tasks that are normally associated with human intelligence, such as understanding natural language, recognizing patterns and objects in images, and making predictions based on data.

B. Types of AI and their Applications

There are several different approaches to AI, including machine learning, deep learning, and computer vision. Machine learning involves using algorithms to learn from data, while deep learning is a subset of machine learning that uses artificial neural networks to model complex patterns in data. Computer vision is a field of AI that focuses on creating systems that can interpret and understand visual information from the world around us.

The use of AI is becoming increasingly widespread in a variety of industries, and its applications are vast, ranging from self-driving cars and speech recognition systems, to recommendation systems that suggest products or services to users based on their browsing history and preferences. As the field of AI continues to grow and evolve, it presents many exciting opportunities for individuals and businesses to make money and improve their operations.

There are several different types of AI and each of them has its own unique applications and potential for generating revenue. Let's take a look at some of the most common types of AI and their applications:

Machine Learning: Machine learning is a type of AI that involves using algorithms to learn from data. This type of AI is used in a variety of applications, including image and speech recognition, natural language processing, and predictive analytics. Companies can use machine learning algorithms to analyze customer data, predict future trends, and automate tasks such as customer service and marketing.

Deep Learning: Deep learning is a subset of machine learning that uses artificial neural networks to model complex patterns in data. It is particularly useful for image and speech recognition, as well as natural language processing. Deep learning algorithms are used in a variety of applications, including computer vision, speech recognition, and natural language processing.

Computer Vision: Computer vision is a field of AI that focuses on creating systems that can interpret and understand visual information from the world around us. It is used in applications such as image recognition, object detection, and autonomous vehicles. Companies can use computer vision technology to improve their operations, for example, by automating quality control processes, or by developing new products and services that rely on visual information.

Natural Language Processing (NLP): NLP is a field of AI that focuses on enabling computers to understand, interpret, and generate human language. It is used in applications such as speech recognition, text-to-speech, and sentiment analysis. Companies can use NLP technology to analyze customer feedback, automate customer service, and improve marketing efforts.

Robotics: Robotics is a field of AI that focuses on creating autonomous machines that can perform tasks in the physical world. Robotics technology is used in a variety of applications, including manufacturing, healthcare, and retail. Companies can use robotics to automate tasks, improve productivity, and increase efficiency.

These are just a few of the many types of AI and their applications. As you can see, AI has the potential to revolutionize many different industries and create new opportunities for individuals and businesses to make money. Whether you are an entrepreneur looking to start a new AI-powered business, or a company looking to integrate AI into your existing operations, there are many exciting opportunities to explore in the world of AI.

C. The History and Evolution of AI

The history of AI can be traced back to the 1950s, when researchers first began exploring the idea of creating machines that could perform tasks that typically require human intelligence. Over the years, AI has evolved and grown in many ways, and has become an increasingly important part of our lives.

In the early years of AI, researchers focused on creating systems that could perform specific tasks, such as playing chess or solving mathematical problems. These early AI systems were based on rule-based systems, in which the machine was programmed with a set of rules to follow in order to perform a specific task.

In the 1980s and 1990s, the focus of AI research shifted towards creating systems that could learn from data and make decisions on their own. This led to the development of machine learning, which is now one of the most important and widely used forms of AI.

In recent years, AI has seen rapid growth and development, driven in part by advances in computing power and the availability of vast amounts of data. The development of deep learning, which uses artificial neural networks to model complex patterns in data, has revolutionized the field of

AI and has led to significant improvements in areas such as image and speech recognition, and natural language processing.

Today, AI is used in a wide variety of applications, ranging from self-driving cars and speech recognition systems, to recommendation systems that suggest products or services to users based on their browsing history and preferences. The use of AI is becoming increasingly widespread in many different industries, and its impact on our lives and the global economy is growing every day.

The evolution of AI has been remarkable, and it is clear that it will continue to play an important role in shaping the future. For individuals and businesses looking to make money with AI, it is important to stay up-to-date on the latest developments in the field, and to explore the many exciting opportunities that AI presents.

D. The Current State of AI and its Impact on Society

AI has come a long way in recent years, and its impact on society is growing every day. The current state of AI is characterized by increasing sophistication and wider adoption across a range of industries.

One of the most notable impacts of AI is its ability to automate many tasks that were previously performed by humans. This has led to increased efficiency and productivity in many industries, but it has also raised concerns about job displacement and the need for workers to acquire new skills to remain competitive in a rapidly changing job market.

AI is also having a profound impact on many other aspects of society. For example, it is being used to improve healthcare by helping doctors diagnose diseases, develop personalized treatments, and make more informed decisions. In the criminal justice system, AI is being used to analyze data, identify patterns, and predict crime, helping law enforcement agencies to prevent and solve crimes more effectively. In the human resource systems, AI is being used to analyze data, identify patterns, and predict employee productivity, helping human resources personnel to limit human element and emotions with hiring and firing employment decisions.

In addition to its practical applications, AI is also having a profound impact on the way we think about and interact with technology. It is changing the way we work, play, and communicate, and it is playing an increasingly important role in shaping the future of society.

Despite its many benefits, AI also presents some significant challenges and risks. For example, there are concerns about the potential for AI to perpetuate and amplify existing biases and discrimination, and the need for safeguards to protect the privacy and security of sensitive data.

The current state of AI and its impact on society highlights the need for ongoing discussions and debates about the role of AI in our lives. It is important for individuals and businesses to stay informed about the latest developments in the field and to consider the ethical and societal implications of AI as they explore its many potential applications.

page break

The Business of AI

Artificial Intelligence (AI) is revolutionizing the way we live and work. The business of AI is a rapidly growing industry with numerous opportunities and challenges. This overview will touch on key aspects of the business of AI, including AI startups and emerging technologies, AI and the job market, AI in different industries, and AI as a service.

A. AI Startups and Emerging Technologies

Artificial Intelligence (AI) is transforming the way we live and work, and AI startups are at the forefront of this transformation. These startups are developing new and innovative technologies that are shaping the future of AI. As the demand for AI-powered solutions continues to grow, investing in AI startups and emerging technologies can be a lucrative opportunity in 2023.

Emerging Technologies in the AI Industry:

Machine Learning: Machine learning is a subset of AI that allows computers to learn from data without being explicitly programmed. Machine learning is being used in a range of industries, from healthcare to finance, to automate tasks and improve decision-making.

Natural Language Processing (NLP): NLP is a branch of AI that deals with human language. NLP technologies, such as chatbots and virtual assistants, are being used to improve customer service and automate mundane tasks.

Computer Vision: Computer vision is a field of AI that deals with the interpretation of visual information. Computer vision technologies, such as facial recognition and object recognition, are being used in a range of industries, including security, retail, and healthcare.

Robotics: Robotics is a field of AI that deals with the design, construction, and operation of robots. Robotics technologies are being used in manufacturing, logistics, and other industries to automate tasks and improve efficiency.

Investing in AI Startups:

Investing in AI software tech startups can be a lucrative opportunity, but it is also a high-risk, high-reward proposition. To increase your chances of success, it is important to conduct thorough research and due diligence before investing. Look for startups that have a strong team, a proven track record, and a clear vision for how they plan to use AI to solve real-world problems.

In conclusion, AI startups and emerging technologies are a promising investment opportunity in 2023. By carefully researching and investing in these startups, investors can tap into the growth potential of the AI industry and reap the rewards. However, investing in AI startups is a high-risk proposition, so it's important to approach these investments with caution and conduct thorough research and due diligence.

B. AI and the Job Market

AI and the Job Market: Navigating the Changes in 2023

Artificial Intelligence (AI) is changing the job market, and this change is only going to accelerate in 2023. AI is automating many tasks that were previously performed by humans, which may result in job losses. At the same time, AI is creating new job opportunities in fields such as data science, machine learning, and AI development.

The Impact of AI on Jobs:

Job Automation: AI is automating many tasks, such as data entry, customer service, and repetitive manual labor. While this automation may result in job losses, it is also increasing efficiency and freeing up workers to focus on higher-level tasks.

Job Creation: AI is also creating new job opportunities in fields such as data science, machine learning, and AI development. These jobs require specialized skills and knowledge of AI technologies, and they offer high salaries and good career prospects.

How to Stay Relevant in the AI Job Market:

Upskill: To stay relevant in the AI job market, it is important to upskill and develop the skills that are in high demand. This may involve taking online courses, attending workshops, or pursuing a degree in a relevant field.

Stay Up-to-Date: It is also important to stay up-to-date with the latest AI technologies and trends. This will help you stay relevant and competitive in the job market.

Network: Networking is key in any job market, and the AI job market is no exception. Building a strong network of contacts in the AI industry can help you stay informed about job opportunities and industry trends.

C. AI in Different Industries

AI in Different Industries: Spotting Opportunities in 2023

Artificial Intelligence (AI) is transforming many industries, from healthcare to finance, and it is creating new business opportunities along the way. By understanding the ways in which AI is being used in different industries, you can identify opportunities for investment and entrepreneurship in 2023.

Healthcare: AI is being used in healthcare to improve patient outcomes, reduce costs, and increase efficiency. For example, AI is being used to develop personalized treatment plans, automate administrative tasks, and assist with diagnosis.

Finance: AI is being used in finance to automate tasks, reduce costs, and improve decision-making. For example, AI is being used to develop personalized investment portfolios, detect fraud, and automate compliance processes.

Retail: AI is being used in retail to improve customer experiences, reduce costs, and increase sales. For example, AI is being used to develop personalized product recommendations, automate supply chain management, and optimize pricing strategies.

Manufacturing: AI is being used in manufacturing to improve efficiency, reduce costs, and increase production. For example, AI is being used to automate quality control, optimize production schedules, and improve supply chain management.

Transportation and Logistics: AI is being used in transportation and logistics to improve efficiency, reduce costs, and increase safety. For example, AI is being used to optimize delivery routes, automate dispatch, and improve safety by monitoring drivers.

D. AI as a Service: Opportunities for Entrepreneurs

AI as a Service: Opportunities for Entrepreneurs in 2023

Artificial Intelligence (AI) is becoming increasingly accessible to businesses of all sizes, and this is creating new opportunities for entrepreneurs. By offering AI services to businesses, entrepreneurs can help companies automate tasks, make better decisions, and improve their bottom line.

Here are a few ways entrepreneurs can make money in 2023 by offering AI as a service:

AI Consulting: Many businesses are looking for guidance on how to incorporate AI into their operations. As an AI consultant, you can help companies identify areas where AI can be used to automate tasks, improve efficiency, and increase profits.

AI Development: If you have the technical skills to develop AI solutions, you can offer AI development services to businesses. This could include developing custom AI models, building AI-powered applications, and integrating AI into existing systems.

AI as a Service: You can also offer AI as a service, allowing businesses to outsource their AI needs without having to hire a full-time team of AI specialists. This could include hosting AI models, providing access to AI algorithms, and offering training and support.

AI Training: Many businesses are looking for training on AI and machine learning, and there is a growing demand for AI trainers. As an AI trainer, you can help businesses understand the basics of AI and how they can use it to improve their operations.

In conclusion, AI is becoming increasingly accessible to businesses of all sizes, and this is creating new opportunities for entrepreneurs. Whether you are an AI consultant, developer, service provider, or trainer, there are many ways to make money in 2023 by offering AI as a service. If you have the skills and expertise, now is the time to take advantage of the growing demand for AI services and make money in the AI industry in 2023.

Investing in AI

A. Introduction to AI Investing

Artificial Intelligence (AI) is one of the fastest-growing industries in the world, and it is creating new opportunities for investors. Investing in AI can be a lucrative opportunity for those who understand the industry and know how to navigate the AI market.

Here are a few key things to keep in mind when investing in AI:

Understanding AI Technology: To be a successful AI investor, you need to have a good understanding of the technology and how it is being used in different industries. This will help you identify potential investment opportunities and make informed investment decisions.

Assessing Market Opportunities: AI is being used in many different industries, and it is important to assess the market opportunities in each industry. This will help you identify the industries where AI is likely to have the biggest impact and where investment opportunities are most likely to be found.

Evaluating AI Companies: When investing in AI companies, it is important to evaluate their business model, technology, and market potential. You should also consider the company's management team, financials, and competition.

Diversifying Your Portfolio: Investing in AI can be a high-risk, high-reward opportunity, and it is important to diversify your portfolio. This means investing in a mix of AI companies, AI-related technologies, and other industries to reduce your overall risk.

Staying Up-to-Date: The AI industry is constantly evolving, and it is important to stay up-to-date on the latest developments and trends. This will help you make informed investment decisions and capitalize on new investment opportunities as they arise.

In conclusion, investing in AI can be a lucrative opportunity for those who understand the technology and know how to navigate the AI market. By assessing market opportunities, evaluating AI companies, diversifying your portfolio, and staying up-to-date, you can make informed investment decisions and potentially earn high returns in 2023.

B. The AI Investment Landscape

The AI Investment Landscape in 2023

Artificial Intelligence (AI) is one of the most promising and rapidly growing industries in the world, and it is attracting a significant amount of investment. In 2023, the AI investment landscape is expected to be more diverse and mature than ever before, offering a wide range of opportunities for investors.

Here are a few key trends to keep in mind when investing in AI in 2023:

AI Companies: Many AI companies are attracting significant investment from venture capital firms, private equity firms, and strategic investors. These companies are developing innovative AI solutions for a variety of industries, including healthcare, finance, and retail.

AI-focused Funds: There are a growing number of funds that are focused solely on investing in AI companies. These funds provide investors with access to a diverse portfolio of AI companies, reducing the risk associated with investing in a single company.

Publicly Traded AI Companies: A growing number of AI companies are going public, providing investors with the opportunity to invest in the AI industry through publicly traded stocks. Publicly traded AI companies offer investors the benefits of liquidity, transparency, and access to larger capital pools.

AI-related Technologies: In addition to investing in AI companies, investors can also invest in AI-related technologies, such as cloud computing, big data, and robotics. These technologies are critical to the development and deployment of AI solutions, and they are expected to grow significantly in 2023.

Emerging AI Markets: Emerging AI markets, such as China and India, are attracting increasing attention from investors. These markets offer unique investment opportunities, as AI is being used to address specific challenges and opportunities in these regions.

In conclusion, the AI investment landscape in 2023 is diverse and mature, offering a wide range of opportunities for investors. Whether you are interested in investing in AI companies, AI-focused funds, publicly traded AI companies, AI-related technologies, or emerging AI markets, there are many ways to invest in the AI industry in 2023. By keeping these trends in mind and conducting thorough research, you can make informed investment decisions and potentially earn high returns in 2023.

C. Choosing the Right AI Companies to Invest In

When it comes to investing in the AI industry, the key to success is choosing the right companies to invest in. With the AI industry growing rapidly, it can be difficult to identify which companies are poised for success and which are likely to face challenges. Here are a few tips to help you choose the right AI companies to invest in:

Focus on Companies with Strong Management Teams: Companies with strong management teams are more likely to have the experience and expertise needed to develop and scale innovative AI solutions. Look for companies with a track record of success and a deep understanding of the AI industry.

Look for Companies with Unique and Scalable Solutions: Companies with unique and scalable AI solutions are more likely to succeed in the long-term. Look for companies that have a clear vision and a solid plan for commercializing their AI solutions on a large scale.

Consider Companies with Strong Financials: Companies with strong financials are more likely to have the resources needed to invest in research and development and to bring their AI solutions to market. Look for companies with a solid balance sheet and a history of profitability.

Invest in Companies with Diversified Revenue Streams: Companies with diversified revenue streams are less vulnerable to market fluctuations and are more likely to be successful in the long-term. Look for companies that have multiple sources of revenue and a diversified customer base.

Consider the Market Potential: Companies that operate in industries with high growth potential and large addressable markets are more likely to succeed. Look for companies that are targeting large, growing markets and that have a clear competitive advantage.

Consider the Competition: Companies that have a clear competitive advantage and that operate in markets with limited competition are more likely to succeed. Look for companies that have a unique value proposition and that have a clear competitive advantage over their peers.

In conclusion, when investing in AI companies, it is important to do your due diligence and to carefully consider the factors listed above. By choosing the right AI companies to invest in, you can increase your chances of success and potentially earn high returns on your investment.

D. Navigating Risks and Challenges in AI Investing

Investing in AI technology can be a lucrative opportunity, but it also comes with its own set of risks and challenges. In order to maximize your returns, it is important to understand and navigate these potential hurdles. Here are some of the key risks and challenges to consider when investing in AI:

Regulation and Ethics: As AI continues to become more integrated into various industries, governments and organizations are starting to establish regulations and ethical guidelines. Failure to comply with these regulations can result in legal penalties, and unethical AI practices can lead to public backlash and loss of consumer trust. It is important to research and stay up to date on the latest regulations and ethical considerations in the AI industry.

Technological Advancement: The AI industry is rapidly evolving, with new technologies and advancements being made all the time. Investing in a company or technology that is quickly becoming outdated can result in significant losses. It is important to invest in AI companies that have a solid track record of innovation and are well positioned to continue advancing in the future.

Data Privacy and Security: AI relies heavily on access to large amounts of data in order to function effectively. Ensuring the privacy and security of this data is a major challenge in the industry. Investing in companies that have a strong track record in data privacy and security is crucial to minimize the risk of data breaches and other security incidents.

Implementation Challenges: Implementing AI technology can be a complex and time-consuming process. Companies may struggle with integration and implementation, leading to delays and potential losses. Investing in companies with a proven track record of successful implementation is key to reducing these risks.

Competition: The AI industry is highly competitive, with many companies vying for market share. Investing in companies that have a clear competitive advantage, such as proprietary technology or a large market share, can help mitigate the risks associated with intense competition.

In conclusion, investing in AI technology requires careful consideration of the risks and challenges involved. By staying up to date on the latest developments in the industry, researching companies thoroughly, and investing in companies with a strong track record, you can maximize your chances of success in the AI investment space.

page break

Making Money With AI

A. Monetizing Your Skills with AI

AI technology has brought about new opportunities for individuals to monetize their skills and turn their passions into profitable businesses. In this chapter, we will explore how you can use AI to make money in 2023.

Freelancing with AI: If you have a skill such as graphic design, writing, or programming, you can use AI to enhance your offerings and stand out in a crowded market. For example, you can use AI tools to generate designs, write content, or automate repetitive tasks, freeing up more time for you to focus on the creative aspects of your work. This can help you increase your productivity and earnings.

Starting an AI-powered business: If you have an entrepreneurial spirit and a passion for AI, consider starting an AI-powered business. Whether it's developing AI applications, offering AI consulting services, or creating an AI-powered product, the possibilities are endless. The key to success is to identify a gap in the market and offer a unique solution that leverages AI technology.

Investing in AI: If you're looking to make money with AI but don't have the skills or experience to start a business or freelance, consider investing in AI. This can be done through stocks in AI companies, or by investing in AI-powered funds or exchange-traded funds (ETFs). Doing your research and staying up-to-date with the latest AI developments can help you make informed investment decisions and potentially see significant returns in the long run.

AI-powered affiliate marketing: If you have a platform such as a blog or YouTube channel, you can monetize it through affiliate marketing and use AI to help you optimize your earnings. AI tools can help you identify the best products to promote, target the right audience, and even predict which products are likely to sell the most, so you can make more money from your affiliate marketing efforts.

By incorporating AI into your skills and business strategies, you can open up new and exciting ways to monetize your passions and make money in 2023. So why wait? Start exploring the limitless possibilities of AI and take your earning potential to the next level!"

B. AI in Affiliate Marketing and Online Advertising

In the digital age, affiliate marketing and online advertising are two of the most popular and effective methods of monetizing a website or blog. With the introduction of artificial intelligence, these methods have become even more sophisticated and profitable. AI has revolutionized the way affiliate marketers and online advertisers approach their craft, and has made it easier than ever to generate income through these channels.

AI in Affiliate Marketing

Affiliate marketing is the practice of promoting someone else's product or service and earning a commission on each sale made through your unique referral link. AI has made it possible for affiliate marketers to automate much of the process, from finding the best products to promote to tracking and analyzing results.

One of the main benefits of AI in affiliate marketing is that it can help you identify the most profitable products and niches to promote. With advanced algorithms and machine learning, AI can analyze data from a wide range of sources, including sales statistics, customer reviews, and competitor analysis, to determine which products are likely to generate the most revenue. This allows affiliate marketers to focus their efforts on the products and niches that are most likely to result in a profit, saving time and maximizing returns.

Another benefit of AI in affiliate marketing is that it can automate the process of creating and distributing marketing materials. With AI-powered content creation tools, affiliate marketers can easily generate high-quality, engaging ads and articles that are optimized for search engines and social media platforms. This helps to increase visibility and drive traffic to the

affiliate website, which can ultimately result in more sales and higher commissions.

AI in Online Advertising

Online advertising is the practice of promoting products or services through digital channels, such as websites, search engines, and social media platforms. AI has transformed online advertising by making it more effective and efficient than ever before.

One of the key benefits of AI in online advertising is that it allows advertisers to target specific audiences with greater precision. With advanced algorithms and machine learning, AI can analyze data on consumer behavior, interests, and demographics to create highly targeted ads that are more likely to result in conversions. This helps to increase the ROI of online advertising campaigns, as advertisers can reach the right people with the right message at the right time.

Another advantage of AI in online advertising is that it can automate much of the ad creation and optimization process. With AI-powered tools, advertisers can easily create high-quality ads that are optimized for search engines and social media platforms. AI can also track and analyze the performance of online ads in real-time, allowing advertisers to make data-driven decisions and optimize their campaigns for maximum efficiency and effectiveness.

In conclusion, AI has revolutionized the way affiliate marketers and online advertisers approach their work. With advanced algorithms and machine learning, AI can help identify the most profitable products and niches, automate the process of creating and distributing marketing materials, and target specific audiences with greater precision. If you're looking to make money in 2023 with AI, affiliate marketing and online advertising are two fields worth exploring.

C. AI and E-commerce: Building an AI-Powered Online Store

Artificial intelligence (AI) is revolutionizing the way we do business. With its ability to process vast amounts of data and make intelligent decisions, AI is increasingly being integrated into e-commerce to enhance the customer experience and increase sales. By 2023, AI is expected to be a crucial component of the e-commerce industry, and those who embrace it will have a competitive advantage. In this section, we'll discuss how you can leverage AI to build an online store and make money in 2023.

Step 1: Choose Your Platform

The first step in building an AI-powered online store is choosing the right platform. There are several e-commerce platforms that integrate AI, including Magento, WooCommerce, and Shopify. Consider the needs of your business, such as the size of your inventory, your budget, and the level of customization you require, and choose the platform that best suits your needs.

Step 2: Invest in AI Tools

Once you have chosen your platform, you can start investing in AI tools that will enhance your store's functionality. For example, you can use AI-powered chatbots to provide customer support and answer frequently asked questions. You can also use AI algorithms to personalize the customer experience by recommending products based on their past purchases and browsing history. These tools will help you increase engagement and sales, and provide a better customer experience.

Step 3: Use AI to Optimize Your Marketing Strategy

AI can also be used to optimize your marketing strategy. For example, you can use AI-powered tools to analyze customer data and create targeted marketing campaigns. This will help you reach the right audience with the right message and increase the effectiveness of your marketing efforts.

Step 4: Utilize AI to Streamline Operations

Finally, AI can be used to streamline operations, making your store more efficient and reducing costs. For example, you can use AI-powered tools to automate repetitive tasks such as data entry and inventory management. This will free up time and resources, allowing you to focus on growing your business.

In conclusion, building an AI-powered online store is a great way to make money in 2023. By investing in the right platform, AI tools, and utilizing AI to optimize your marketing strategy and streamline operations, you can increase sales, provide a better customer experience, and stay ahead of the competition.

Artificial intelligence (AI) is rapidly changing the Software tech industry, offering numerous opportunities for investors to make money in 2023 and beyond. AI is helping to streamline processes, improve decision-making, and drive innovation in the Software tech sector. In this section, we'll discuss the ways in which AI is transforming real estate and how investors can take advantage of these opportunities.

Step 1: Invest in AI & Software tech Companies

One of the most straightforward ways to invest in AI Equity is to invest in AI & Software tech companies. AI & Software tech companies are technology-driven startups that are revolutionizing the software industry by using AI and other cutting-edge technologies to solve real problems. By investing in these companies, you can be a part of the growth of the AI & Software tech industry and potentially profit from the success of these companies.

Step 2: Invest in Equity, Stock or Hedge Funds with AI Focus

Another way to invest in AI in real estate is to invest in Equity, Stock or Hedge funds that have an AI focus. These funds typically invest in stock or equity assets that are being transformed by AI, such as properties with smart home technology, properties with AI-powered energy efficiency systems, and properties that are being managed using AI-powered property management systems. By investing in these funds, you can gain exposure to the growth of the AI real estate industry while also benefiting from the traditional benefits of investing in real estate.

Step 3: Invest in AI-Powered Software Startups

Another option for investors is to invest directly in AI-powered Software startups. By investing in these startups, you can be a part of the growth of the AI real estate industry and potentially profit from the success of these companies. However, it's important to do your due diligence and thoroughly research the startups you're considering before making an investment.

Step 4: Invest in AI-Powered Software Products

Finally, you can invest in AI-powered Software products, such as smart home systems, AI-powered energy efficiency systems, and AI-powered property management systems. By investing in these products, you can be a part of the growth of the AI Tech industry and potentially benefit from the success of these products.

In conclusion,

AI is transforming the Tech and Software industries, offering numerous opportunities for investors to make money in 2023 and beyond. Whether you choose to invest in AI & Software tech companies, equity funds with an AI focus, AI-powered tech startups, or AI-powered tech products, the key is to stay informed and stay ahead of the curve. By doing so, you can potentially profit from the growth of the AI Software industry while also benefiting from the traditional benefits of investing in technology companies.

www.ingramcontent.com/pod-product-compliance
Lightning Source LLC
Chambersburg PA
CBHW072147230526
45467CB00040B/784

* 9 7 9 8 3 8 6 1 9 9 4 8 7 *